Leon's Story

understanding diabetes

Shaganappi Community Health Centre
3415 - 8 Avenue S.W.
Calgary, Alberta
T3C 0E8

Monique Lanouette, Nurse
Suzanne Douesnard, Psychologist
Monique Gonthier, Pædiatrician
Angèle St-Jacques, Nurse

Illustrations by Melina Di Cristo

A first edition of *Leon's Story* has been published in 1990
by Hôpital Maisonneuve-Rosemont under the title *La Petite Histoire de Léon*.

Illustrations: Melina Di Cristo

Computer graphics: Nicole Tétreault

Production : Éditions de l'Hôpital Sainte-Justine
 3175, chemin de la Côte-Sainte-Catherine
 Montréal (Québec) H3T 1C5
 Phone : 514 345-4671
 Fax : 514 345-4631
 www.hsj.qc.ca/editions

Legal deposit: Bibliothèque nationale du Québec, 2005
 Library and Archives Canada, 2005

Dear parents

Your little one has diabetes. Since the diagnosis was made, you've felt upset, concerned, sad and angry. Although you feel helpless and confused, you must also understand this disease and learn how to control it.

Moreover, you must be more available and attentive than ever to your child's new physical and emotional needs. That's a lot to ask! Yet, the emotional storm will calm, the upheavals will be less intense and your suffering will ease. Adaptation will stay its course.

Leon's Story has been designed to help children with diabetes understand what is happening to them and to help parents provide the support they need.

Just as understanding diabetes will help you adapt to the situation, your child must also understand in order to accept the requirements of the treatments and cooperate with them. A child who understands can ask questions, discuss, negotiate and take part in the treatments rather than passively deal with the disease. Even a very young child can grasp the importance of the disease and it's treatments and recognize the emotions they stir.

With Leon, you can also help your child to recognize his or her emotions and provide much needed reassurance. This way, your child and you will learn together not to reject pain and anger but to give them their just place without allowing them to become overwhelming.

This book is a tool that we are offering you. We are still available to accompany you and your child and their sisters and brothers, as well as those around you. (...)

Instructions

This book has been designed for preschool children, but it can also be of use for older ones. In fact, the explanations must be repeated frequently since the child is constantly changing in terms of emotional and intellectual development.

If your child is a baby, you can start showing him or her images and books. Draw your child's attention to the pictures in *Leon's Story*, using very simple words to name the important elements in the image and miming actions or emotions with voice and gestures. Just as diabetes is a part of your child's life, *Leon's Story* can also be a part of his or her library. If your child has started speaking, he or she can comment the words and the pictures and you can encourage this activity. You should adapt the story to your child's level of understanding.

At the age of 4 or 5, your child can understand *Leon's Story* as it is written, but still needs help reacting and talking about his or her own experience.

We hope that your child will grow with Leon and that this imaginary diabetic little boy will become friend.

Others

Leon has a sister who must also adapt to the changes in her family's life. She too expresses her emotions. If you have other children, you can get them involved in reading the book, encourage them to react, ask questions and express their feelings. As in the case of the diabetic child, they need to understand the situation in order to adapt to it better.

This book can also be used to help grandpa and grandma, a cousin, the babysitter and your child's friends, who will also be upset and want to understand and help.

Enjoy your reading, let this book entertain you, and don't forget to welcome pleasure in your daily life.

Suzanne Douesnard

5
◆

For a few days, Leon hasn't been himself.
He's always thirsty...

... and he goes to the washroom more often.

He's always hungry. He's starving.

He feels tired and listless. His sister Rosie finds him boring because he never wants to play like he used to.

Today, he's going to see the doctor,
with his mother and Rosie.

Dr. Martin examines him and explains that they
will have to take blood tests to find out what's wrong.

The nurse takes some blood from his arm.
Have you ever had a blood test?
For Leon it was his first time.

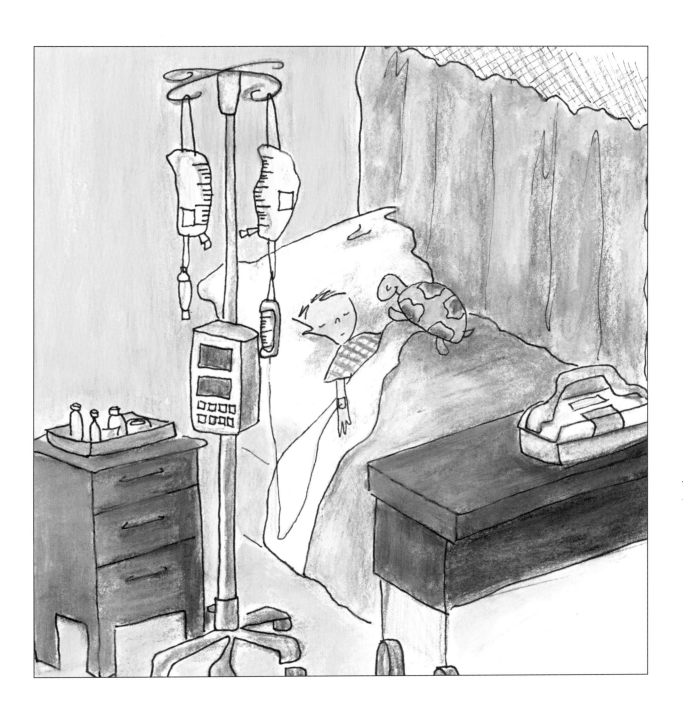

Leon has to spend a few days in the hospital.
His turtle, Bertha, is with him. To help him feel better,
the hospital staff gives him medicine
through a long tube connected to his arm.

The next day, he already feels much better,
but he wonders what's going on. They tell him
that he has *diabetes*. Is it because of the chocolate
he ate at grandma's house? Not at all!
It's because his pancreas is sick.

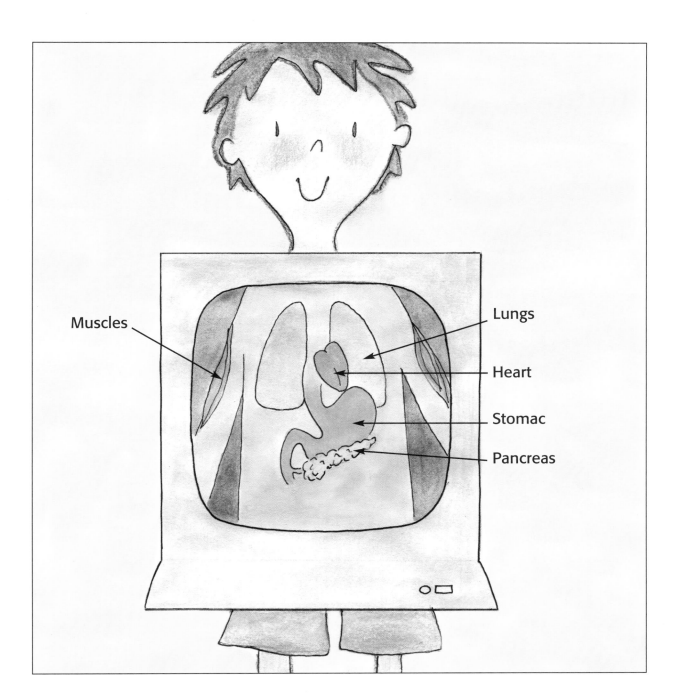

Muscles

Lungs

Heart

Stomac

Pancreas

Leon learns that people have a *pancreas* right there,
in their tummy. If we could look inside the body
with a special TV... we'd see that we have...
*a heart that beats... lungs to breathe...
a stomach that digests food... a pancreas that makes
insulin, muscles to move... and lots more...*

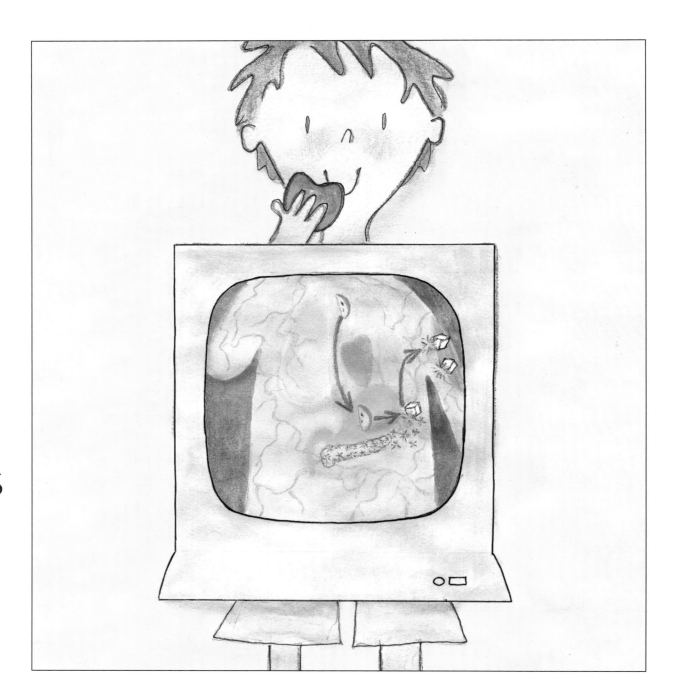

In your tummy, the stomach and your pancreas work
together. The stomach takes the food you eat and changes
it into sugar. The sugar travels through the blood, throughout
your entire body, right into your muscles. The pancreas sends
little crystals of insulin to catch the sugar and help it provide
the energy that keeps you feeling good.
You see what happens with the bits of apple...
It's like that with many other foods we eat.

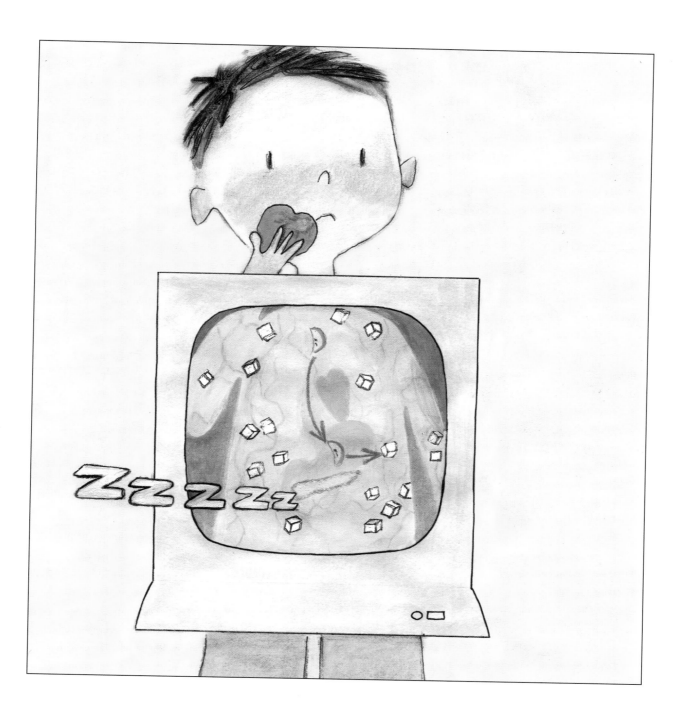

If we could look into Leon's body with a special TV,
we'd see that his *pancreas is sick.*
It's sleeping. ZZZZZZZ... It doesn't make insulin
anymore. The sugar travels alone without its friend
insulin. So, the sugar can't change into energy and
that's why there is too much sugar in Leon's blood.
That's what happens when you're diabetic!

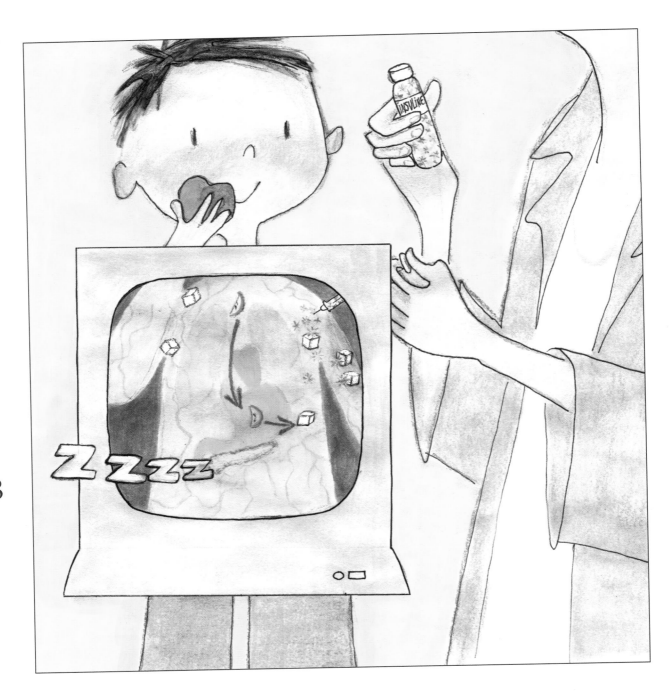

Fortunately, Leon gets insulin injections. The little crystals of insulin meet up with the sugar and *everything goes back to normal*. Leon feels good like before and he's full of energy to move, run, jump and have fun, even if his pancreas is still sleeping.

Leon feels good again and wants
to play ball with his friends.

**They need a ball to play with.
Do you want to draw one for them?**

It's important to know how much sugar is in the blood to make sure there is just enough. To do this, you have to *prick* your fingertip several times a day. Older people call this *checking their sugar*.

Sometimes, Leon is asked to pee in a little pot.
Leon finds this embarrassing. This is to find out
if there is *acetone* in his urine. What a funny word!
It's a good thing Daddy and Mommy understand!

Leon's parents spend a long time talking with the
nurse, the doctor and the dietician. Leon would like
to know how they find so much to say. Sometimes
they're sad and upset by everything that's happening.

Leon likes it when they explain to him
what's happening, too. It's all so complicated!
Hypo? Hyper? Soon, he'll understand it all better.

Leon doesn't really like *needles*.
Sometimes he cries and says it hurts.
Sometimes, he's more afraid. Suzy taught him
some tricks to take his mind off the needles,
like blowing bubbles...

... counting to 4 or reciting a rhyme...
See, it's already over! Do you know any other tricks
to make you less afraid and make it hurt less?

26

At the hospital and at home, Leon's parents can give the injections as well as the nurse can. Leon makes sure his skin is clean before the injection.

Sometimes, Leon chooses the spot for the injection.
His arm? His thigh? His buttock?
Sometimes, they use a syringe, sometimes
a funny device that looks like a pen.

Leon likes to play giving injections.
"You're a diabetic too, Bertha, and I'm taking care
of you!" "If you want to stay healthy, you have to eat
good food, like the lettuce you like so much."

Leon will be healthy when he eats good food
for his meals and snacks every day... just like Daddy...
like Mommy... like Rosie and his friends.

Leon has to eat fewer sweets.
Sometimes, it's allowed, but only when Daddy
and Mommy say so. *Sometimes means
"not very often"*. It's a good thing there are
a lot of good foods and good desserts to eat.
Rosie and Leon both go wild over them.

At the grocery store, Leon can help his mother choose good foods. Do you want to help, too?

Choose the foods that Leon should put in his basket.

32

When Leon runs or moves a lot, his muscles work hard
and his body needs more food. His parents have
to learn to balance it all with Leon.

That's why Daddy gives him a big snack when they
go on an outing. Daddy likes snacks, too.

Sometimes, Leon feels "funny".
He may feel dizzy, shake and have a headache
or a stomach ache. He may also feel really hungry.
What's happening? He doesn't have enough sugar
in his blood and his body is sending him a message.
"You must eat", says a little voice.

Leon must stop playing right away and tell
the adult who is taking care of him. After drinking
some juice, he soon feels better.
A little snack and he can keep on playing.

Do what Leon does. Draw a picture of you
when you have low blood sugar.

When Leon has low blood sugar, he knows that he must drink some juice. Drinking **3 ounces or 90 millilitres of juice** is like a treatment for low blood sugar.

At home, Leon gets a lot of attention.
Grandma sometimes brings him surprises
"just for him". "Leon, always Leon." Rosie is fed up!

Leon goes home to check his sugar.
Rosie is happy because it gives her a chance
to finish her snowman all alone with Mommy.
She thinks her brother isn't all that lucky...

39

When Leon went back to daycare, his friends
were glad to see him. The daycare worker also knows
what to do if Leon says he doesn't feel well.
Daddy and Mommy explained diabetes to her.

41

Leon and his friends are having a great time,
just like before. Find what's funny in the drawing.

Since he feels better, Leon thinks that he is cured.
He doesn't understand why he's "still diabetic".
Why is this happening to him? Sometimes it makes him sad,
sometimes very angry. Daddy explains it's just really
bad luck and no one's fault... Leon likes rocking
in Daddy's arms before going to sleep.

Leon goes back to the clinic often to see the doctor and the entire team. He's not afraid of the injections and can check his sugar himself. But, sometimes, *he doesn't want to hear any more about diabetes. He doesn't want to hear people say, "There's no choice." He doesn't want to see another needle for the rest of his life and he wants to eat lots of candies.* His parents understand and talk about it with him.

44
◆

At the clinic, there are a lot of other children
with diabetes. Some small, some big.
Bruno says that he does his own tests
and uses a super pen for his injections.
Leon understands that he will always be diabetic,
even when he's big like Bruno.

Bruno shows Leon a photo of a camp for kids
with diabetes where he now works as a counsellor.
"You can come, too, when you're bigger."
Leon doesn't know if he'll go,
but he thinks it could be really fun!

Leon is happy because, even if he has diabetes,
he can still have lots of fun every day with his friends
and his sister Rosie. That's what counts!

Novo Nordisk is proud to support Leon and all people living with diabetes.

For more information on Novo Nordisk and how we can help you and your child with diabetes, visit our website at www.novonordisk.ca

novo nordisk®